graveyard tulips

Emil Claire

Presentation by *BookLeaf Publishing*

Web: www.bookleafpub.com

E-mail: info@bookleafpub.com

ISBN: 9789360949358

First edition 2024

To blueberry muffin,

for teaching me the word 'bookworm'.

ACKNOWLEDGEMENT

I would like to thank the most important person in my life without whom none of this would be possible, myself. Writing anything is hard so I'm proud of myself for taking this huge leap and trying new things.

Honestly, there aren't a lot of people I have to thank or particularly appreciate as this was a very small-scale project that I trusted in the hands of like, five(?) people.

So thank you to my Amma, who has been encouraging me to write ever since she found my first 'top secret story' because, without you, I wouldn't have done any of this. I guess you can say 'I told you so' for the rest of my life now.

And to my sister for being my first test audience and reader. Coolest big sister ever.

Last but not least, my grandmother, who inspired my first ever poem. I guess you're my muse.

Also, this collection may not be what many consider poetry, and that's okay, but it's my style of poetry and I like it.

August.

That day had been a rainy one.
The rain reminded me of you.
What they said, it made no sense
it couldn't be true.
I looked up, a house made of cards
home no longer felt like you.
Back when every story was new
now turned hazy and blue.
Words uttered, prayers known
all those people yet so alone.
One umbrella, two souls
every drop reminded me of you.

With your pink slippers and warm smile,
your round glasses and arms wide,
the way you scrunched your nose,
disapproved of my vice.
A flower blooming,
the angel of doom.
A father crying,
a family consumed.

Stardust and glitter,
fairies galore,
I still keep that snow globe,
if anything but to cope.

My childhood mere colors
but they will always be hers.
A woman sleeping,
her dreams preserved.
My broken heart,
now reserved.

Love is all a child deserves.

Kuro Neko

People are so queer,
saying things with such fear
'You mustn't cross that ladder!'
lest you be madder.
Don't roll that dice,
for you might sink twice!
There shall be no umbrellas inside
Dear man, forget your pride!
Clutching their hearts,
swallowing despite.
What funny little people,
what a funny little sight!

The Dreamer

She was a little girl,
with little dreams.
She would be a thief,
with her little schemes.
Maybe a baker, any takers?
She could be an artist, use some paper.
Be a detective, no one could escape her.
Or she could be a gardener,
plant some flowers in a bed
and they would be oh so red!
A pilot in the skies,
making up all kinds of lies.
Perhaps, a doctor saving lives?
Be like a librarian,
oh how wise.
A spy, master of disguise.
A villain plotting someone's demise.
She could be anything or everything,
if she tried.

Me and I

Little me, what do you think is love?
What we see in the movies, that's not us.
Do you think love is kind?
do you think it's warm?
do you think I would agree?
Because that's not what I see.
I miss who I used to be,
like you, but more like me.
Have I lost my glow?
hidden in the snow.
Pretending to dazzle
to not lose my castle.
You wouldn't agree,
because that's not what you see.
I wish to be free,
go back to being we.

He's just a man

When she asks where I've been,
I said, "Out getting revenge."
Looking at my blood-soaked gown,
she gives me a smile.

When the townsfolk hear the news they say,
"It's been about time."
They saw it coming down from a mile.
The cops don't bother making a case file,
the news stations pretend to be hostile.

We sip tea and don't even bother to lie,
he was never really worth the time.
Everyone knew he'd had it coming for a long
while.
Everyone knew it was me all the while.

Hide and Seek!

Monsters lurking in the house
you keep fleeing like a mouse.
Lock the doors, hide in the bed.
While they paint the walls blood red.

love, me

To love is to
understand
that it doesn't
change anything.
Being loved
is to realize
that it doesn't mean
everything.

I need a hug

How does one know
the warmth of love,
whilst living under a roof
with no affection?

wishing well

Standing in the remains
I wonder to myself
what I would give
to go back
to my childhood days.

chapter one

Sadness is the feeling you get

after finishing a book

that was never meant to be read.

Bittersweet is the ending

for a heart that will not mend.

blueberry muffin

Flour and sugar, milk and eggs
enough to feed all three heads
a pinch of salt, whisk with no halt
set in a tin, batter thin
add the berries with child-like merry
spoon the batter, fill the tray, no scatter
bake in the oven, the secret coven
toothpick in the heart, dough clean
as they come out gold and purple,
one can hear three voices interpel.

russian roulette

A vile of poison, a table of six,
glasses of wine, sneaky tricks
secrets spilling, tainted lips
an intent to kill, the clock ticks
a fallen body, a silent mix
the role of a lifetime, the game begins.

daddy's little girl

Princesses don't cry
they smile with puffy eyes.
Little girls always yearn,
parents unconcerned.
"You are just a prize"
don't go thinking twice.
All those pretty lies,
are dreams that slowly die.

strawberry crush

Pink cheeks and cloudy skies,
two kids just passing by.
A full moon in late July,
you took me by surprise.
Calling me by my name,
how do I explain?

Sunshine on a rainy day,
you smile and I melt away.
There goes my mind,
making me blind.
It's just a phase,
part of a summer haze.

Soon I'll be awake,
see that it was fake.
So I play this game
and I'm the one to blame
when it goes to flames.
Maybe it's my fate,
who is yet to say?

Act I

Deep breaths, longing stares
standing here, looking there.
Take a step, face the glare
have no care, don't be aware.
Nothing's as bad as it is in your head.
They don't know, trust it shows.
Fake a smile, there she goes.

Bright lights now feel like home,
self-assured from head to toe.
Take a step, the air feels rare.
There's no care, she's not aware.
Things worked out better in the end.
And as she smiles, she does glow.
After all, it's just a show.

flower

'how was your day?'

standing outside,
drenched in the rain
a flower in your palm,
with a smile so mundane.

a feeling arises I can't quite explain.

pinky ponky

remember when
you were so small
your toes fit the bed?
remember when
life felt like a fairytale
you had just read?
remember back when
you were clueless and
had nothing in your head?

because I do, and I'd do it all again.

fairy cottage of mine

It'd be shaped like a mushroom
with its red little head.
One little window to sneak in a spread,
Old wooden furniture, books fill the bed,
A friendly stray kitten there for the bread,
And me with pure bliss and no sense of dread.

Dear diary,

I hope one day I meet someone like you
someone who listens, through and through.

the tiles are green

wet bathroom floors, mattress depression
locked all the doors, should I let them in?
as the tears pour, I wonder in silence,
'where did I go, and why didn't they notice?'

i adore you

other matters apart,
you stole my little heart,
with all your charms and wit,
even the most peculiar bit,
that's right, I've fallen for it all.

The Great Indian Romance

she's all alone
in the house
she calls home.
should've just ran
now she's stuck
with a man.
expecting no love,
just push and shove.

'welcome to marriage,
there's no special carriage.'

upside window view

the sun is hiding,
while the clouds dance their little dance,
the car is gliding,
while the statues stand their little stance.
i am smiling,
while my eye blinks its little blink.

the winner takes the crown

I wish I didn't care
so much about
everything .
Maybe then
I wouldn't feel so
guilty for how little
I do .

teenage drama queen

She likes the color pink,
reading magazines so she
doesn't have to think.

She only talks about boys,
drama she simply enjoys.

She's very superficial,
kind when beneficial.
She's truly a monster beneath it all.

happiness is like a pair of keys, i still search for it

After the tears have dried
and the room is now quiet,
I wonder what it is like
to be someone who never tried.

A jar of hyacinths

anger is that bedtime story that was never
finished,
sadness is knowing that the moment has passed,
hope is the coin you threw in that fountain,
fear is a partner on the other side of the bed,
loneliness is waiting for the happy end,
and happiness is the rainbow you wish would
never bend.

I was my last love

what a shame it is
that people spend
their whole lives
looking for a soulmate
when no one
could compare to them.

gripping the groceries

As I walk my way home,
beneath the gloomy skies,
stepping on the charred rocks
across the slimy road,
I smile, because it's a holiday.

we found solace under the stars

I like being alone
but don't go
I like being alone
with you too

I am more than my pain, so is my art

sometimes hurt is just hurt
it's not art
it's just hurt
and that's okay.